D0938798

What Do You Like?

What

Michael Grejniec

Do You Like?

HARCOURT BRACE & COMPANY
Orlando Atlanta Austin Boston San Francisco Chicago Dallas New York
Toronto London

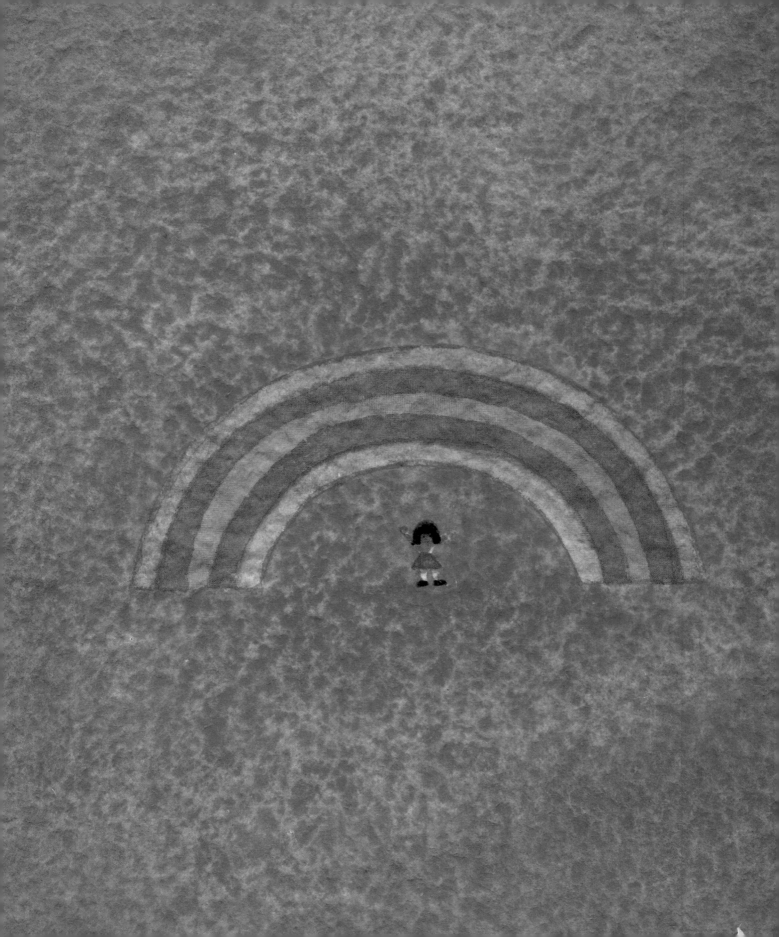

I like the rainbow.

I like the rainbow, too.

I like to play.

I like to play, too.

I like my cat.

I like my cat, too.

I like fruit.

I like fruit, too.

I like music.

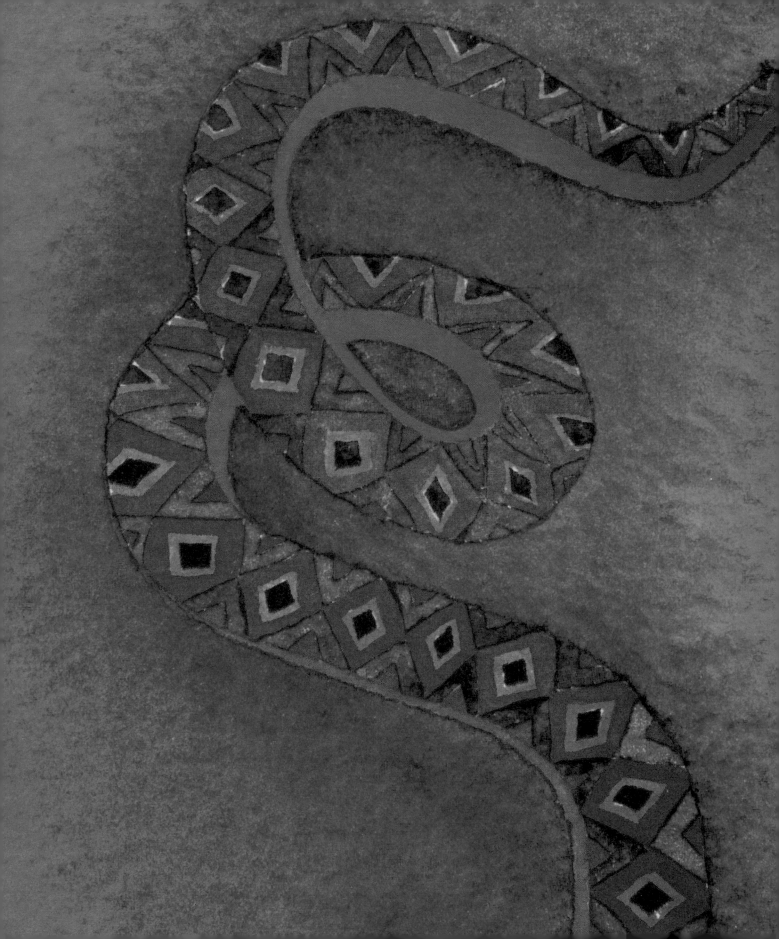

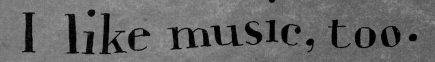

I like music, too.

I like to fly.

I like to fly, too.

I love my mother.
I love my mother, too.

What do you like?
What do you love?

This edition is published by special arrangement with North-South Books Inc.

Grateful acknowledgment is made to North-South Books Inc., New York, for permission to reprint *What Do You Like?* by Michael Grejniec. Copyright © 1992 by Michael Grejniec.

Printed in the United States of America

ISBN 0-15-302119-5

4 5 6 7 8 9 10   035   97 96 95